Adventures and Other Silly Things

Lakisha Edwards

BookLeaf Publishing

India | USA | UK

Presentation by *BookLeaf Publishing*

Web: www.bookleafpub.com

E-mail: info@bookleafpub.com

ISBN: 9789360949396

First edition 2024

*This book is dedicated to my daughters,
Alexis, Elisha, and Nakia.*

Friends

Tried and true
Conversations below the surface
Laughs non-stop, tears unashamed
Carefree silliness and inside jokes
Shared memories that tickle for decades
So glad to have met, whenever that was
Meeting or calling for the first time in years, yet
feeling like I saw you yesterday
It feels like we've always known each other

Teachers' Friday Night

2

Hard work is hard work...hard work, work!

Monday was MLK Day; a day to celebrate a
leader of non-violent protests
Tuesday was a school district meeting about
reacting to gun violence

Wednesday night parents received notice of a
potential 1/19 shooting threat
Thursday was 1/19, so we taught the 60% that
were present

Friday, was Career Day with assemblies, guests,
and speakers
Friday night is exhausted teachers intending to
grade papers...zzzz

Monday

Seated at a table in the cafeteria surrounded by
peers
Pretending not to be hungry, while holding back
tears
Tummy cramping, hoping no one hears it growl
Because the Friday cafeteria lady said, "No food
for you, if you can't pay now."
A concerned teacher call me over and asks,
"What's the deal?"
Why aren't you eating? Why don't you have a
meal?"

"My mama is a homemaker and papa hasn't
worked in weeks.
I haven't told anyone because I'm too shy to
speak."

The teacher is silent for a second, but doesn't
miss a beat
saying, "Go on about your day, but I'll make sure
you eat."
Little did I know, she reported this immediately.
The counselor called my house and confirmed it
all with Mami.

The teacher shared this with her team peers, and because they care a bunch
the next day the cafeteria lady said, "You've got enough on your account for two weeks of lunch."

Safety

Safety is not a guarantee, its a feeling
Where I work, where I shop, where I relax,
where I worship
Safety is not a guarantee, its a feeling
I feel safe, but safety's not a guarantee
In the desert of Iraq, 13 months with a weapon
on my side 24/7
Safety is not a guarantee, its a feeling
Wear your seatbelt, look both ways, don't talk to
strangers

Teaching curious students with questions about
the police in the building
after a violent threat written on the boys
bathroom stall
I give them freedom to ask questions and discuss
possible scenarios
I can't guarantee their safety, but I can make
them feel safe enough to focus on learning today
Safety is not a guarantee, its a feeling

We can plan, practice drills, and arm ourselves
to a "T"
we can fear the negative possibilities and stay
hidden indoors

We can live life to the fullest or at least be
grateful for small things each day
Take care of ourselves and or loved ones the best
way we can
Safety is not a guarantee, its a feeling

It's My Birthday

Next week is my birthday and I want to do it big
for 49
Not "big" in the traditional sense, but big in
quality time
My budget's tight, so I won't spend too much
cash
I want to spend this day with fun friends, the
ones that make me laugh

I have several close friends, but I can't invite
them all
Sold me house in the divorce and my new
apartment is quite small
The invitees will be the girlfriends that know all
my dirt
So I'll find a way to make the seating and the
roominess work

Besides, they really know me and are wonderful
friends of mine
They'll celebrate with me and everything will be
fine.
"Your presence is my present. Bring a dish.
Casual is the dress."

My birthday's not just another day and spending
it with dear friends reminds me that I'm blessed.

Food, fun, and games will be the agenda.
I'm so looking forward to a birthday to
remember.

But

My days are busy, but it's honest work.

My week is tiring, but rewarding.

My "clients" at work are unpredictable, but the work is also tedious.

The pay here is better than most in my position, but not much for the local cost of living.

I don't want to quit, BUT I NEED MORE MONEY.

My application for an easy part-time job positions are received, but denied.

I know what I want form me, but I gave in and asked God to place me where He needs me.

He said, "Give your time, but have no expectation of pay."

That wasn't my goal, but I obeyed and began volunteering.

That same week I got a random email from an
association I'd taken classes with years prior,
but why?

It was an offer for a well paying part-time
position.
...but God!

Traffic

If I had all the time in the world
this is not where I'd choose to be.

Move! Watch out! Get out of the way!
It's like all the city's drivers are in the same place
at the same time.
I'm running late, so I'll put the blame on you.
Yes, you! The driver ahead of me who doesn't
have a clue.

Move ahead, fill in the gaps. Stop wasting
inches on the highway.
I've got places to go and people to see. This is
contributing to my anxiety.

A red car signals she want to change into my
lane.
Letting her in will cost me 30 seconds, and I
can't be late again.

Road rage is real. It's inside every one of us.
I'm four miles from my destination, but the GPS
says 20 minutes.

Inhale. Exhale. Positive thoughts. Don't go insane.
This would all be find and dandy if everyone would just stay in their lane!

Hips

I want to try something new. Something fun, just
for me.
Not too hard, but not too easy. Make a friend,
maybe three.

Salsa lessons! Class schedule and the cost are
perfect, just right.
It says here, "One free trial lesson." Oh, I'm
starting tonight!

One, two, three. Four, five, six. Moving hips to
the rhythms they play.
Celia Cruz, Tito Puente, and others from back in
the day.

Level one for beginners is calming, yet good
aerobic exercise.
Signed up for twice a week. In one month, I
delighted in the inches lost in my thighs.

"This new thing is a confidence booster", I think
as I sashay out the studio door.
You better believe, I'll be coming back for more.

Auf Wiedersehen

So long, farewell, auf wiedersehen, good-bye!
A professional trip across the world, way on the
other side.

To elevate my profession and experience a new
culture, as well.
What adventures will await me? Only time will
tell.

The largest country in central Asia, and ninth in
the world to be exact.
Most of my family and friends have only heard
of it from Borat.

The people dress like westerners, and the
majority look Asian.
In the big cities, they speak Russian, yet most
practice the Muslim religion.

A 10-hour time difference will make phone calls
challenging with friends and family.
Thank goodness for WhatsApp, Google Voice,
and other communication technology.

This may be a once in a lifetime experience, or
the start of something new.
The last two years, I started the application, but
then doubted what I could do.

I'm grateful my sister encouraged me to actually
complete my third application.
Is the third time a charm? Or was this all in
God's timing?

VIP

Fancy name placards, glass waters bottles and
drinking classes
A microphone for each person placed in front of
each seat
Paparazzi-like cameras flashing
Videographer recording from various angles in
the room
Fellowship contract signed
University rector and Embassy reps, too.
Exchange of the cultural gifts and handshakes
Look at these very important people
What? Who? Me, too?!

FOMO

I'm bored. Let me check Facebook.

I am sitting in the waiting room. Let me check
my emails.

I have a 20-minute bus ride. What's new on
Instagram?

I'm standing in cashier number 3's line. Do I
have new text messages?

I made a tasty dinner, took the perfect pic of it,
and posted it. Let me see how many folks like it.

I'm so tired and ready for bed. But, I'll just
make one last check of FB, my emails, my
Instagram account, and text messages because I
may have missed something.

Hospitality

No smiles as we pass, just a nod.

Curious glances, but out of respect no staring.

Another day of straight faces the whole route home. Poker faces, tired faces, resting b— faces.

The elderly woman next door surprisingly smiles upon seeing me entering my apartment.

She's speaking words and asking questions that I can't comprehend. I say the only thing I know in her language, "My name is Lakisha." She giggles.

She pulls out her cell phone, types something, then shows me. "Come for tea at 7pm tonight."

How sweet! How hospitable! Plus it was just nice to see a smile.

At 7, I arrive to a buffet of food, snacks, and sweets.

So many options and a beautiful display.

Any empty plate or cup was quickly refilled.

With our phones and translation app, we had a
full conversation and got to know each other.

I didn't know an invitation to have tea would be
such a sweet cultural exchange and warm
display of hospitality!

Taxi Ride (Every single one)

Seat belt? What for?

Are you from India or Africa?

Oh, America?! I love America!

New York, yes?

Oh, Georgia. Near Miami!

I have a relative that lives in America.

What do you think of my beautiful country?

What is your job here? English teacher?!

Can you give me and my children lessons?

What do you think of the cuisine?

How old are you?

Beshbarmak

We eat what we know, and we know what we
eat.

A different country's cuisine may not be such a
treat.

But how do you know, if you've never tried?

Just thinking about it makes me lose my
appetite.

Yes, I know that on special occasions this is your
traditional dish.

But I'm only familiar with beef, pork, chicken,
and fish.

You seated me at the head of your table, because
I am the oldest and honored guest.

So, tonight will be the night I put this meal to
the test.

It looks appetizing enough, I just have a mental
block.

All eyes on me…hmmm…it's not bad…

…mmm, I do like Beshbarmak!

Teacher's Workshop

It's not about you, it's not about me.

It's about helping the students be the best they
can be.

I'm not here to judge, just to share what I know.

If we work together and keep open mind, the
workshop exchange will flow.

Let me show you some English language
teaching strategies.

A few will be new, but you may already use
some of these.

Everyone up and out of your seats!

You'll role-play as students and I'll I think this is
perfect model methodology.

Switch things up, let students speak and move.
Give them repetitive tasks to gain knowledge
they can prove.

Now you have a bag of academic activities to
reference
and both your students and you are steadily
gaining confidence.

Issyk Lake

Green hills that peak as snow-capped mountains
A turquoise lake with water still and clear
Plants in bloom, but slowly fading to make room
for the next season

Yellow, red, and orange covers the mountain
side
The lake shines, still and clear
No seasonal plants remain
The chilly air announces autumn

Winter blankets the mountain range
Trees peek through, standing tall in white veils
Beneath the frosted mirror lies the tortoise lake
waiting patiently for spring

Tacos, Burgers, and Mac & Cheese

I miss burgers and Mexican food.
Your restaurants try, but they never taste as good.

I miss the seasonings, the textures, and flavors.
Just to taste the real deal is what I savor.

I give your version another chance and order it again.
Maybe a different restaurant or menu item.

No, that didn't do it for me. It's still not the same.
You just cook it differently; no one's to blame.

I try to make it myself but can't find all the ingredients.
I guess I'll make it myself, with a bit of a twist.

Nope! Still not hitting. I'm done. I'll just wait…
'til I'm back across the ocean in the United States.

Smack That

Oooh, the profanity! Did you hear what he just
said?
There are children and families here, and the
song lyrics are pretty bad.
This song has lots of cussing and suggestive
overtones.
It seems inappropriate here, over coffee and
scones.

The loudspeaker plays a rapper's explicit details
of how he makes his lady smile.
While I'm just trying to find fresh produce in
this supermarket aisle.

At first I was shocked. Now it's kind of a comic
treat.

That's right, you don't speak the singer's
language, you just enjoy the beat.

The Constant

Hearing your voice on the line brings comfort
Today was a whirlwind of mishaps and
miscommunication
You understand

Hearing about your day keeps me grounded
It reminds me of the normalcy of familiar people
and places
Your heart is my home

Hearing your rational perspective
When I become unfocused in an idea or a plan
When I'm anxious about the possible variables
You are my constant

God's Love

I can feel it in the hugs from family and close
friends
I can feel it in the chilly breeze or warm sun of
the four seasons

I can see it in the magnificent shades and hues of
all living things
I can see it in a 90-year old's smile as well as in
the adorableness an infant brings

I can hear it in the birds' songs at the break of
dawn
I can hear it in "I forgive you," when I've done
something wrong.

It's all around me, even when I'm not paying
attention
And just in case I failed to mention

It's for each of us, in every part of the world
Each day find something to be grateful for

Express your gratefulness to Him up above
And know that you're never ever without God's
love